D0207576

To a
Very Special
Friend
on Your
Birthday

Blue Mountain Press ®

Boulder, Colorado

To a Very Special Friend on Your Birthday

A collection of poems
Edited by Robin Andrews

Library of Congress Catalog Card Number: 90-83141
ISBN: 0-88396-285-3

ACKNOWLEDGMENTS appear on page 62.

design on book cover is registered in
U.S. Patent and Trademark Office.

Manufactured in the United States of America
First Printing: October, 1990

Blue Mountain Press ®

P.O. Box 4549, Boulder, Colorado 80306

CONTENTS

7   Lindsay Newman

8   Deanna Beisser

10   Susan Polis Schutz

12   Denise Johnston

13   Janet S. Allen

15   Susan Polis Schutz

16   Collin McCarty

19   Dan Carr

20   Betsy Gurganus

23   Collin McCarty

24   Luann Auciello

27   Jane Alice Fox

28   Deanne Laura Gilbert

29   Alin Austin

31   Chris Gallatin

32   Rodger Austin

35   Deloras Lane

36   Garry LaFollette

39   Ron Hiser

40   Donna Levine

43   Susan Polis Schutz

44   Ben Daniels

45   Denise Johnston

47   Sheryl Skutelsky

48   Collin McCarty

50   Brenda Neville

52   Carey Martin

54   Brian Bindschadler

56   Collin McCarty

58   Laura Medley

60   Donna Levine

62   Acknowledgments

Birthday Wishes for a Very Special Friend

There are so many things
  I'd like to say to you today . . .
like how much your friendship
  means to me,
and that I hope we'll always
  be friends.
I'd like to thank you for all
  the wonderful things you've
    ever done for me
and for all the times you've
  been there when I really
    needed someone.
I'd like to list one by one
  all of the special qualities
    you possess,
but that would take too long.
So instead I'll just wish you
  the best birthday ever,
and many, many more to come!

—Lindsay Newman

Happy Birthday
to Someone Special. . . You

Special people are those
who have the ability to share
  their lives with others.
They are honest in word and deed,
they are sincere and compassionate,
and they always make sure that
  love is a part of everything.
Special people are those
who have the ability
to give to others
and help them with the changes
  that come their way.

They are not afraid
of being vulnerable;
they believe in their uniqueness
    and are proud to be who they are.
Special people are those who
allow themselves the pleasures
of being close to others
    and caring about their happiness.
They have come to understand
that love is what makes
    the difference in life.
You are a very, very special person
who truly makes a beautiful difference
    in this world.

—Deanna Beisser

You Are a Perfect Friend

You have known me
in good and
bad times
You have seen me
when I was happy
and when I was sad
You have listened to me
when what I said was intelligent
and when I talked nonsense

You have been with me
when we had fun
and when we were miserable
You have watched me
laugh
and cry
You have understood me
when I knew what I was doing
and when I made mistakes
Thank you for
believing in me
for supporting me
and for always being ready
to share thoughts together
You are a perfect friend

—Susan Polis Schutz

Your Friendship Has Made
a Difference in My Life

(2)

Every year our lives are filled
with different challenges, successes,
  and some failures;
every year we travel down different roads
  and meet different people
  and have different dreams.
Every year makes a difference in our lives.
You are always there for me,
no matter what day or what year.
Sharing with you
all that is important to me
has made a difference in my life.

As you celebrate your special day,
and you look back over the last year
and forward to the days that lie ahead,
I want you to know
that I hope I can make a difference
  in your life
by being your friend,
as you have done for me.

—Denise Johnston

There is so much I
want to give you...

On this special day,
   and always,
I wish I could give you
all the good things
that life has to offer.

But since I can't,
I will give you what I can —
   encouragement
   in whatever you do,
   joy in what you accomplish,
   sharing in your dreams,
   hope for your future,
   and friendship and love,
   now and always.

—Janet S. Allen

A Birthday Thought
for a Wonderful Friend

Sometimes we are lucky enough
to meet a person who stands out
among all the other people
as being extremely special
who knows what we
are thinking about
who is happy for us at all times
who is always there to talk to us
who cares about us selflessly
who is always truthful with us
Sometimes we are lucky enough
to meet someone who is
extremely wonderful
For me
that person
is you
my dear friend

—Susan Polis Schutz

It seems like I'm always searching
for a way to tell you
how wonderful I think you are.

And I thought that maybe
on your birthday
I could convey a little thought
   that I would love to say to you . . .

You're my definition of a special person.

I think you're fantastic. And
exceptional and unique and endearing.
To me, you're someone
who is very necessary to my well-being.
In so many ways, you fill my life
with happiness and the sweet feelings
of being so grateful and appreciative
   that you're here.

I could go on and on . . .
   but you get the picture.

I think you're a masterpiece.

—Collin McCarty

Happy Birthday to You

Today is the day to celebrate
the birth of someone very special:
someone who continues
to bless the lives
   of so many others
just by being there;
someone who gives a smile,
   a helping hand,
caring, and concern.
Today is the birthday
of someone who seeks to be
a person of trust,
who listens and advises;
someone who is always there
when others turn away;
someone who brings joy
into the world;
and who is an inspiration,
   a helper, and a friend.
Today is the birthday
of someone very special
   and dear to my heart.
And that someone is you.

—Dan Carr

Let's Never Let Go
of Our Friendship

(3)

I don't ever want us to let go
of each other.
Maybe our paths will go
in separate directions,
but that won't change the bond
we share and what's in our hearts.

No matter where I am
or what I am doing,
when you come to mind
a smile comes to my face
and a warmth settles in my heart.

The day you and I met
will always be cherished.
We've grown together,
done a lot together,
and no matter what,
we always let each other know
that we do love and care
about each other.
You are more than just
    a friend to me.

I often struggle to say how I feel,
but I hope we never let go
of what we share,
because whether it's across the miles
or just a short distance,
you are and will always be
a part of my life and me.

—Betsy Gurganus

These are the birthday gifts
I wish for you . . .

Happiness. Deep down within.
Serenity. With each sunrise.
Success. In each facet of your life.
Close and caring friends.
Love. That never ends.

Special memories. Of all the yesterdays.
A bright today. With much to
    be thankful for.
A path. That leads to beautiful tomorrows.

Dreams. That do their best to come true.
And appreciation. Of all the wonderful
        things about you.

—Collin McCarty

A Friend Is One of Life's Most Beautiful Gifts

A friend is a person you can trust,
who won't turn away from you;
a friend will be there
when you really need someone,
and will come to you
when they need help.
A friend will listen to you
even when they don't understand
or agree with your feelings;
a friend will never try
to change you,
but appreciates you for who you are.
A friend doesn't expect too much
or give too little;
a friend is someone you can share
dreams, hopes, and feelings with.
A friend is a person you can think of
and suddenly smile;
a friend doesn't have to be told
that they are special,
because you both feel that way.
A friend will accept your attitudes,
ideas, and emotions,
even when their own are different,
and will hold your hand
when you're scared.

A friend will be honest with you
even when it might hurt,
and will forgive you
for the mistakes you make.
A friend can never disappoint you,
and will support you
and share in your glory.
A friend shares responsibility
when you have doubts.
A friend always remembers
the little things you've done,
the times you've shared,
and the talks you've had.
A friend will bend over backwards
to help you pick up the pieces
when your world falls apart.
A friend is one of life's
most beautiful gifts.

—Luann Auciello

There's no time like a birthday
to let someone know
just how cherished they are.

You've been such a
wonderful friend to me,
and on your birthday
I just want you to know
how grateful I am
for your friendship.
There are not many true friends
that enter one's life,
but when one does,
we grab hold and never let go.
You, my dear friend,
will remain treasured
in my heart forever.

—Jane Alice Fox

A birthday is a time
for counting blessings,
and I want you to know
that I consider our friendship
one of my greatest blessings.
Together, we've built a relationship
that is strong and enduring.
We've consoled each other
and stood by each other.
Our friendship has truly been
a cherished gift,
one that always will remain with us.

I am thankful for all
that we have meant to each other
over the years.
You have touched my life
in so many ways,
and your friendship is a gift
I will always cherish.

—Deanne Laura Gilbert

To My Very Special Friend...

I want your birthday to be so happy
  and so wonderful for you!
May it bring you . . .
the treasure of memories made;
the beauty of dreams and hopes;
the thankfulness of blessings received;
the feelings of worth and wonderfulness;
the experience of new paths to travel;
the promise of tomorrows yet to unfold;
and the smile that comes from
      knowing . . .
  that I hold you in my heart so dearly.

Thanks . . . on your birthday and all
  through the year . . . for being such
    a wonderful friend . . . to me.

—Alin Austin

A birthday is a day of happiness,
a day for sharing feelings,
and a time for celebrating
   a very important person.

And *your* birthday is
   an especially important day . . .
because it's a time to wish you a
   wonderful year ahead.
And it's a time to wish you a treasure
of happiness from the year gone by.
And it's a time to wish you
   a lasting reminder that you are
      very special to me . . .

   and you always will be.

                              —Chris Gallatin

I Feel Especially Blessed
to Have You for a Friend

People come and go in our lives,
but some cross our paths and leave
a lasting impression that lives
    in our memories forever.
They touch us in a special way
that changes us for the better
    and makes us grow.

My friend,
to realize what you have done for me,
to realize how you have given me
    a part of your life
    and shared all the times,
    both good and bad,
is to feel blessed in a special way.

To share this special day with you
is more a gift to me than anything
    I could ever give to you,
and maybe sharing it together
is what giving is all about.
I hope my giving you
my love and appreciation
    on your birthday
will let you know just how
very special you are to me.

—Rodger Austin

On your birthday,
look back and remember
all the happy times
  in your life.
Cherish those memories
of days gone by.
Look ahead and dream
of all the bright possibilities
  your future holds.
Nurture those hopes and plans
  for tomorrow.
Look at your life now,
and give yourself credit
for all you've accomplished.
Then celebrate your birthday
for all it's worth,
and enjoy every single
  minute of it!

—Deloras Lane

My Birthday Wishes for You

I hope that your life is always filled
with the joy of friends and family,
and that each day brings you
the pleasures and deep rewards
of love and friendship.
I hope that your heart is always at peace,
that in unsteady and uncertain times
you will always have something to
hold on to as a source of comfort
and peace in your thoughts,
your beliefs, and your life.
I hope that your efforts are
always rewarded, and that you
experience the joy of achievement
and always have the excitement
of meaningful challenges.

I hope that you'll always find
the things that matter most to you,
that your responsibilities
will still leave you with the time
　　and freedom for
the people and activities
that provide your deepest satisfaction.
I hope that the end of every journey
provides a chance for reflection
and appreciation for everyone
who helped you
and for everything you gained
along the way.

—Garry LaFollette

May All Life's Best Be Yours
on Your Birthday and Always

May life always bring much pleasure,
   enjoyment, and contentment
   to you,
and even in the trying times,
may life be as gentle with you
   as it is possible to be.

May life never rush you,
   but give you time
to think about what is happening,
   to understand it, and
      to learn from it.
May life always touch you
the same way you touch others:
   with gentleness,
   with caring,
      with love.

—Ron Hiser

Birthdays Are a Measure
of Growth Through the Years

Life is a constant process
of growth and change.
Each day is a miracle filled
with new discoveries
and challenges.

Birthdays are a measure
of life's growth —
in experience,
in courage and
    compassion,
in love and strength.

Birthdays are a time to consider
changing your life to make it
    more meaningful to you,
changing your attitudes,
and staying flexible about everyday living.
Life will keep getting better
as long as you have
a positive attitude.

Each day, remind yourself
of all the things you love about life,
stay in touch with your
loved ones and friends,
and do what your own heart tells you.
Tomorrow will always bring you good things
if you live each day with love.

—Donna Levine

There are so many things
to do each day
There is so much going on in the world
of great concern
that often we do not stop and think about
what personally is really important
One of the nicest things in my life
is my friendship with you
and even if we don't have a lot of time
to spend with each other
I want you to always know
how much I appreciate you
and our friendship

—Susan Polis Schutz

Every year
when it's time for your birthday,
I find myself thinking
about the times we've shared
and the wonderful memories
we have of each other.
We have been good friends
for quite a long time now,
and it's such a nice feeling
to have a friend who
knows me so well
and whom I know so well.

I hope you have
a great birthday
and a year ahead
filled with a lot
of great things.

—Ben Daniels

I am so glad that,
as the years have come and gone,
our friendship has stood strong.
We have travelled
down the roads of our lives;
at times, we have
hung on to each other
for strength and support
through the tears and trying times;
at other times, we have shared
the happiness in our hearts.
I am so proud
to have you for my friend;
I want you to know how special
you truly are to me.

—Denise Johnston

For Your Birthday,
My Friend

For your birthday, I simply wish
that you could receive
all the things you give to others.
I wish you true friendship,
which you always offer.
I wish you peace and happiness,
which you always convey.
And most of all, I wish for you
a life filled with joy and love,
because I know that you, my friend,
have given so much love
to so many other people.

—Sheryl Skutelsky

You're My Crazy, Warm, Wonderful Friend... and I Don't Know What I'd Do Without You

I've got a few special words
I'd like to share
with you . . .

To you, my friend:

For keeping my spirits up.
For never letting me down.
For being here for me.
For knowing I'm there for you.

For bringing so many smiles my way.
For being sensitive to my needs.
For knowing just what to say.
For listening better than anyone else.

For bringing me laughter.
For bringing me light.
For understanding so much about me.
For trusting me with
    so much about you.

For being the best.
For being so beautiful.

I don't know what I'd do
    . . . without you.

—Collin McCarty

When a Special Friend
Comes into Your Life . . .

Once in a while a special friend
comes into your life
and touches you in a wonderful way.
Your personalities just seem to click,
and it seems as though your friendship
has existed for years.
Immediately there is a sense
of trust and sincerity,
and a feeling of closeness
develops instantly.

Once in a while somebody special
comes into your life,
and right away you know
you have found a friend.
Even after parting,
this person leaves such an impression
that from time to time, for no reason,
you think of that friend,
  and it makes you happy.

—Brenda Neville

A birthday
is a time when
we are free to say
some of the things
that we wouldn't
   ordinarily say
      to someone
         we care about.

So I'll take advantage
   of this time to say . . .
that I wish you
   much more
than just a
   happy birthday.

I wish you happiness
   each and every day,
in return for all the joy
   you bring to life.

I can't begin to thank you
for everything; my simple words
don't do you justice.
But my heart knows how I feel,
   and maybe you do, too.

For I feel as though
today is not just a day to
wish you a happy birthday;
   it's a day to celebrate
      everything about you.

—Carey Martin

A Friend
Is a Part of You Always

Friendship is a special gift
given to us all.
The smile of a friend
is sunlight on a cloudy day,
and every smile given to a friend
   is returned.
A friend is
one whom you can talk to,
   and listen to,
      without judging.

A friend doesn't ignore your faults
but accepts them as a part of you.
A friend is a shoulder to lean on
  when you need support,
a pat on the back when you do well,
and a sympathetic ear when you fail.
A friend is a person
you can laugh with
  about everything,
you can cry with without shame,
and whom you trust completely.
A friend is a partner in life
  and a part of you always.

—Brian Bindschadler

On Your Birthday,
and All the Year Through,
May You Remember
These Things I Wish for You

May you know, in your heart, that
  others are always thinking of you.
May you always have rainbows that
  follow the rain.
May you celebrate the wonderful things
  about you.
And when tomorrow comes, may you
  do it all over again.

May you remember how full of smiles
  the days can be.
May you believe that what you search for,
  you will see.
May you find time to smell the flowers,
  and find time to share
    the beauty of you.

May you envision today as a gift
   and tomorrow as another.
May you add a meaningful page to the
   diary of each new day,
   and may you make
   "living happily ever after..."
   something that will really come true.

And may you always keep planting
   the seeds of your dreams.
      Because if you keep
         believing in them,
      they'll keep trying their best...
         to blossom for you.

                              —Collin McCarty

To My Very Good Friend

We have all had many friends
throughout our lives,
but only a few of those friends
we would call good friends.
That's because being a good friend
involves time
and understanding
and love,
which can be difficult to share
with another.

When I think of my good friends,
I always think about you,
because that is what you have
   been to me.
You have taken the time
to be there when I needed you,
and you have listened to me
when my life was changing.
You have always cared enough
to try to understand my feelings
and help me to understand myself.
And, most important,
your consideration and honesty
have shown me
that your friendship is true . . .
symbolizing a very special kind
   of love
that only a few friends
ever share with one another. (1)
Thank you for being such
a good friend to me,
and for all the joys we have known
together.

—Laura Medley

My Birthday Wish for You, My Special Friend

A friend like you is a special gift . . .
We like to do so many of the same things,
and we share a lot
    of wonderful, fun moments.
You respect me for my strengths,
as I admire you for yours.
We encourage each other
during our difficult times,
and laugh with each other
during our good times.
I know I can be myself with you.

A friend like you is a precious gift . . .
We can tell each other
our secret dreams and desires,
cheer each other on to
more success and happiness,
and wipe each other's tears
when we are sad and disappointed.
You are a bright light in my life,
and you have a special place in my heart.

On your birthday,
I want to wish you all your best
dreams come true,
and that you have success and happiness,
a fulfilled heart, and laughter.
And I want to tell you that
you are beautiful to me,
and I cherish our friendship.

—Donna Levine

ACKNOWLEDGMENTS

The following is a partial list of authors whom the publisher especially wishes to thank for permission to reprint their works.

Denise Johnston for "Your Friendship Has Made a Difference . . . ." Copyright © 1990 by Denise Johnston. All rights reserved. Reprinted by permission.

Jane Alice Fox for "There's no time like a birthday . . . ." Copyright © 1990 by Jane Alice Fox. All rights reserved. Reprinted by permission.

Rodger Austin for "I Feel Especially Blessed . . . ." Copyright © 1990 by Rodger Austin. All rights reserved. Reprinted by permission.

Deloras Lane for "On your birthday . . . ." Copyright © 1990 by Deloras Lane. All rights reserved. Reprinted by permission.

Ron Hiser for "May All Life's Best Be Yours . . . ." Copyright © 1990 by Ron Hiser. All rights reserved. Reprinted by permission.

Donna Levine for "Birthdays Are a Measure . . . ." Copyright © 1990 by Donna Levine. All rights reserved. Reprinted by permission.

Sheryl Skutelsky for "For Your Birthday, My Friend." Copyright © 1990 by Sheryl Skutelsky. All rights reserved. Reprinted by permission.

A careful effort has been made to trace the ownership of poems used in this anthology in order to obtain permission to reprint copyrighted materials and to give proper credit to the copyright owners. If any error or omission has occurred, it is completely inadvertent, and we would like to make corrections in future editions provided that written notification is made to the publisher:

BLUE MOUNTAIN PRESS, INC., P.O. Box 4549, Boulder, Colorado 80306.